STEAMBOAT VISIONS

A PHOTOGRAPHIC VIEW OF THE YAMPA VALLEY

STEAMBOAT VISIONS

KAREN SCHULMAN

•

JOE RIFE

Introduction by

Lynne Greco

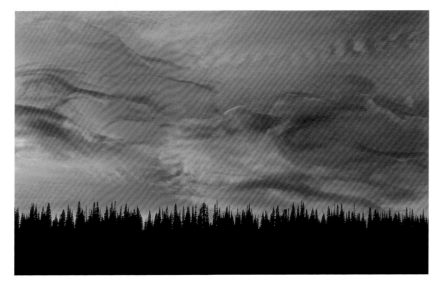

A unique perspective of lifestyles,

landscapes and personalities

of the Yampa Valley.

ICON Press, Inc.

Steamboat Springs, Colorado

In memory of my mother, Mina Rustin, for her continuous encouragement in all of my creative endeavors.

Joe Rife

To the memory of my parents, Harriet and Joseph Gordon, for teaching me to see.

Karen Schulman

Publisher

Icon Press, Inc.
P.O. Box 770304
Steamboat Springs, CO 80477
303-879-2244 Voice and FAX
303-879-7838

Text and photographs copyright ©1993 by Icon Press, Inc.
Cowboy Poetry copyright ©1993 by Bill May.

First Edition
Library of Congress Catalog Card Number
93-61287
ISBN 0-9638546-0-7 softbound
ISBN 0-9638546-1-5 hardbound

Printed in the United States of America by Paragon Press, Inc., Salt Lake City, Utah.

This book was designed using QuarkXPress on an Apple Macintosh computer.

Printed on Potlatch Quintessence Dull Book and Cover. Text is set in Nofret Light and Nofret Light Italic.

Any inquiries regarding the photographs may be directed to Icon Press, Inc.

Editing and Design: Joel Schulman
Design Consultant: Laurie Fetterolf
Captioning: Joanne Palmer
Proofreading: Sandy Lindsay

Acknowledgements

To all in our family and our "family of friends", thank you for your support and understanding during the *Steamboat Visions* project. We also graciously thank everyone who has given permission to include, in the book, photographs of themselves, their children, pets or property. Special recognition goes to Joel Schulman for countless hours of assistance in editing text and photographs and for an incredible design job.

In addition, we wish to give special thanks to the following people who gave so generously of their time, energy and expertise: Sue Beauregard, Dick and Leslie Ryan, Laurie Fetterolf, Joanne Palmer, Vern and Lynne Greco, Fritz Aurin, Al Fairbanks, Sandy Lindsay, Bill Malone and Nancy Kramer.

Sincere thanks to Bill May for allowing us to reproduce his beautiful poetry.

introduction

*G*azing out over the Yampa Valley from the west side of Rabbit Ears Pass, one can see for countless miles. It's a breathtaking and inspirational sight. The vista seems limitless, creating a feeling of immense space, nurturing ambitious dreams and exuberant spirits. The serenity of the gentle mountains and the meandering river on the valley floor create a relaxed and hospitable attitude in the people who live in Steamboat Springs.

This big western valley infuses all who enter it with an expansive feeling. We pride ourselves on being neighborly, family-oriented, adventurous and independent. Our heritage of working the land and being a community long before we were a resort, lends a genuineness and a commitment not often experienced in a resort town. While we wrestle with the challenges inherent in growth and development, we continue to maintain a can-do attitude which fosters cooperative efforts and a generosity that I have found to be unparalleled.

Our active lifestyle is a direct reflection of the appreciation we feel for the great fortune of living here. Winter dumps mind-boggling amounts of snow and challenges everyone to participate. Shades of cool blue and soft white fill the horizon. Spring brings a yearning to be outdoors in the gradually warming days. High country flowers burst open displaying a mosaic of rich colors. Summer finds us reveling in the glorious sunshine whenever possible as we pursue our favorite activities. A warm and somewhat frenzied feeling radiates as we make the most of long days and seemingly endless sunny skies. Autumn precipitates a slower pace and a savoring of the diminishing daylight. Dazzling golds and fabulous yellows emblazon the landscape with breathtaking beauty.

We love the lives we have made here. Our feelings about Steamboat Springs go beyond words. The photographic images on the following pages capture more completely the essence of this extraordinary place and bring *Steamboat Visions* to life.

Lynne Greco,
Past President, Steamboat Springs Arts Council
Board Member, Colorado Council on the Arts
and longtime Steamboat Springs resident

Snow blankets the Yampa Valley and
the slopes of Mt. Werner, delight-
ing visitors and residents alike.

Anyway you look at

it, Steamboat is

Ski Town, USA!

The best skiers in the world meet to compete in Steamboat,

from local Winter Sports Club racers to national and

international World Cup competitors.

There's more than one way to get down

the slopes in Steamboat. You can

race, jump or bump like Steamboat's

own Nelson Carmichael.

Olympic Medalist, Nelson Carmichael

Sometimes after a hard day

on the slopes you just

feel like ganging up on

your instructor.

Flying, Steamboat style!

Cowboys trade in their horses but keep their chaps on for a day on the slopes at the Cowboy Downhill.

Billy Kidd, Steamboat's Director of Skiing

What seems so simple in summer can often be a little trickier in winter, particularly after one of Steamboat's legendary snowfalls.

A solitary moment skiing on Steamboat lake.

Speaking of the early days in Steamboat..."You parked your truck as soon as the first snow and left it parked until May. You got around on horseback, on skis or with a team and sled. That was the only way of transportation."

Clarence Wheeler
Local Rancher

Hahn's Peak

Fun takes to the streets in the oldest continuing

winter carnival west of the Mississippi.

This is the time of year when locals and

ranchers join together to celebrate winter in

the mountains.

The Steamboat Springs High School Band

Going...

going....

A shovel has more

than one use in

Steamboat.

gone!

Joe Pete LoRusso recovers!

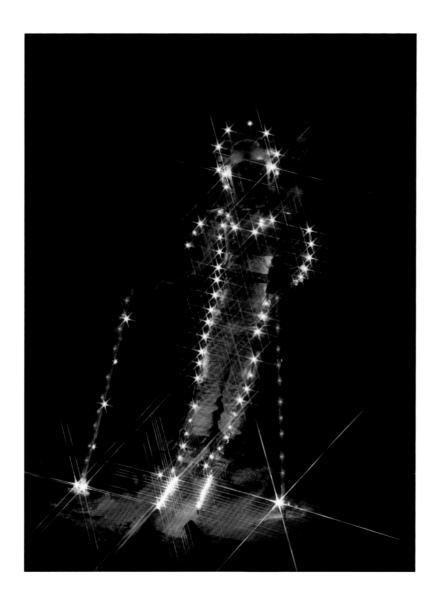

Kids, don't try this at home! Claudius Banks first lit up the night

in his innovative costume in 1936. His son Jon continues the

family tradition, flying in from Washington every year to ski

down the slopes of Howelsen Hill as "The Lighted Man."

Spring fever is contagious...

causing locals to jump

into jello, ski in swim

suits and build crazy

crafts from cardboard.

Spring arrives...

... and with it come the beautiful

alpine wildflowers.

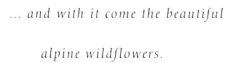

Colorado Columbine

Indian Paintbrush and Lupine

Fireweed

48

Steamboat

Lake

Rabbit ears...

...sheep ears.

53

Pleasant Valley before the Stagecoach Reservoir dam

There's more than one way to enjoy

the water when the snow melts.

The start of the annual Rubber Ducky Race

It's a dog-day afternoon.

During high school I worked as a soda fountain jerk at the old Kinney Drug. Steamboat was so small back then that if we saw a new face in town, it was either someone's visiting relative or a tourist. The most asked question by visitors was, "What do people do around here?"

I hadn't ever given it much thought. My friends and I never seemed to be hurting for entertainment. To me, we had lots of things to do...like ride up Rabbit Ears with friends and go skiing. Or play hide and seek at twilight in the woods behind our house. Or saddle up Yukka Bukka and bounce around for awhile. Or go camping with my family at Hahn's Peak.

Sometimes we'd spend afternoons at the pool. Or watch another western movie at the Chief Theater. Or we'd march our earnings across Lincoln Avenue to The Dorothy Shop (she gave me my first charge account when I was fifteen). Or we'd go to the football game because everyone was there. The Friday night dances during the summer were the best! Kids from all over Routt County attended. We also square danced in tournaments around the state.

In winter there was ski practice four nights a week and our coach made us sidestep up the course (instead of riding the lift). He said that we'd get in better shape. We did!

So, when I was asked, "What is there to do around here?", sometimes all I could say was, "how about a snowball fight?"

Sue Beauregard

View of Sleeping Giant and downtown Steamboat Springs

4th of July Parade, Lincoln Avenue

Balloon Rodeo, Rainbow Weekend

The arts come to life in Steamboat.

Dal

Leck,

Moonlight

Smithy

Lisa

Koch,

Clay

Artist

Bill

May,

Cowboy

Poet

Peter

Van De Carr,

Part-time

Musician

Racing takes to the streets

of Mt. Werner during

Vintage Auto Weekend.

Steamboat Motorcycle Week

Vintage Airplane Fly-In

Fall colors on the slopes of Mt. Werner

A peaceful end to a

beautiful day.

Night lights, Routt County

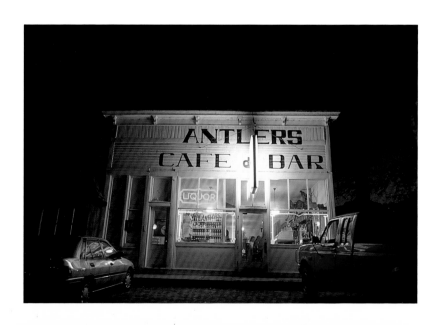

Vern Greco on Indy

"There is something omnipotent in the spirit of the American west...something that captures a part of almost everyone who spends any time here. Steamboat Springs and the Yampa Valley manifest that spirit!"

Vern Greco
President, Steamboat Ski and Resort Corporation

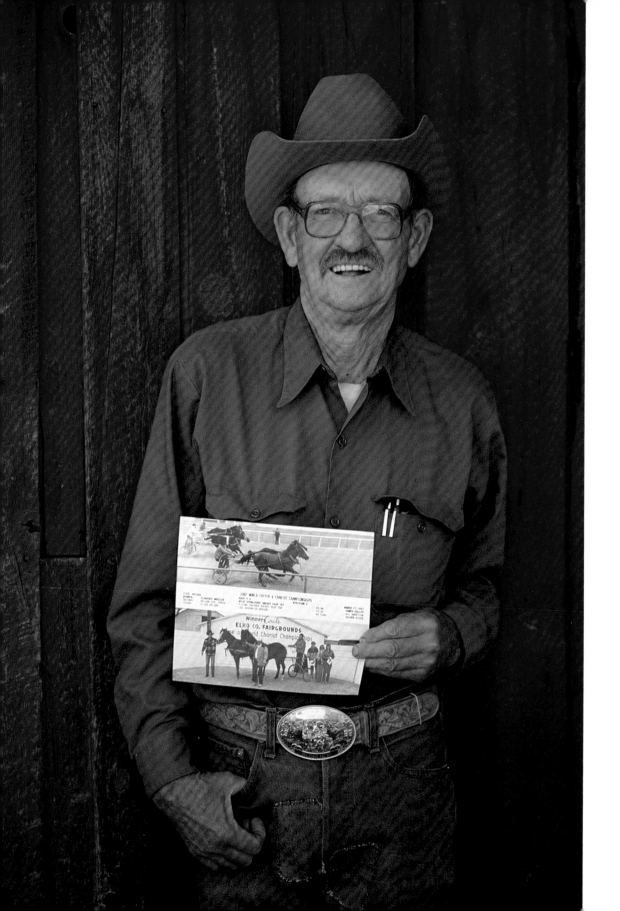

Ranching has its roots in the

Yampa Valley. Two of

Steamboat's hard working

ranchers, Clarence and

Ruth Wheeler.

Terry

Klein,

Cowboy

Pat

Mantle,

Legendary

Cowboy

Jim Dorr

The Sombrero Stables horse drive is the last of its kind

in the country. Every spring over 600 horses are

moved from their winter pasture to their summer

homes. In the fall, the drive is reversed, providing

a true glimpse of the old west.

Brent Romick, President,

Steamboat Springs

Pro Rodeo Series

Bucking broncos, clowns and near

disasters keep rodeo audiences

riveted all summer long.

Banjo

The future of the west is

in their hands.

How grand those days when I was young and free

And rode the range without a fret or care.

I long again to hear the melody

Of freight - train - whistle on the autumn air.

We drove the cattle to the loading pen;

Sometimes one thousand head – and even more.

And, Oh! The glory of the drive back then;

When cowboys trailed to rail, in days of yore.

And when the cars were loaded and pulled out

We rode the old caboose, and how we sang.

We passed around the jug with many a shout;

And how the echoes in the tunnel rang.

So, now, as I approach the Great Divide --

I listen for the whistle as I ride.

Bill May

Cowboy Poet and Rancher

Neil Hummel, Rodeo Judge